GOD
A.K.A. JESUS CHRIST

Richard S. Schofield

Copyright © 2007 by Richard S. Schofield

GOD A.K.A. JESUS CHRIST
by Richard S. Schofield

Printed in the United States of America

ISBN 978-1-60034-569-2
ISBN 1-60034-569-7

All rights reserved solely by the author. The author guarantees all contents are original and do not infringe upon the legal rights of any other person or work. No part of this book may be reproduced in any form without the permission of the author. The views expressed in this book are not necessarily those of the publisher.

Unless otherwise indicated, Bible quotations are taken from the King James Version. Copyright © 1988 by B.B Kirkbride Bible co., inc.

www.xulonpress.com

Table of Content

Foreword 5
Dedication 7
Who's on Fire? 9
New Testament 15
It's All in the Family 19
Doubting Thomas 23
The Road to Damascus 27
I Am 33
The Word 37
Mount Of Transfiguration 39
The Mystery of Godliness 41
Fashioned as a Man 45
What Happened on the Cross? 47
Who was Melchisedec 49
The Godhead: What Is It? 53
Alpha and Omega 55
Who Sits on the Throne? 59
That Rock Was Christ 65
The Great Wrestling Match 69
Jesus Standing on the Right Hand of God 71
Summary 75

God Can, God Did, God Will..................................77
Jesus Only, Only Jesus...81
Author's Biography 83

Foreword

Praise the Lord to all who open these pages to read what thus sayeth the Lord. I do hope that all of you who may read this book may find some solace in your search for a better understanding. However this book will probably not convince those that are not filled with the Holy Ghost, that Jesus indeed is God almighty. I will, if the Lord permits, speak to you in a book that is yet to come. However at this juncture God has led me to address those that are spirit filled but yet do not believe that Jesus is God. 1st Corinthians 12:3 declares…that no man can say that Jesus is the Lord, but by the Holy Ghost , so according to 1st Corinthians the Holy Ghost will reveal to you who Jesus Christ really is. I understand that there are millions of you across this universe that has been filled with the Holy Ghost, but you are undecided about who Jesus is. For lack of a better description allow me to call you apostolic fence sitters you are sitting atop the fence only because a more perfect way has not been expounded to you. In Acts 18:26 Aquila and Priscilla took Apollos aside …and expounded unto him the way of God more perfectly. I do not think your position is entirely your fault. I will not be addressing this issue from a "know it all" view point. This book is directed by the auspices of the Holy Ghost, and I could only write as I was moved by the Holy Ghost. I refuse to write based on theory because theory is based on conjecture and conjecture is based on faulty evidence. Now when theory and conjecture are removed that leaves truth standing alone, and for truth we turn to John 17:17 …thy word is truth. The holy scripture is our source of revelation of who Jesus really is, we use only scripture to verify our belief that Jesus Christ is really God almighty. Before you read any further please pray and ask God to open up your understanding and your discernment, it won't be this book that brings revelation, but as is written in 1st Corinthians 12:3…but by the Holy Ghost.

Dedication

This book is devoted to Christians everywhere who have fought and struggled with family and love ones, who just can't see that Jesus is God Almighty. I will only attempt to name a few of those that have helped in some way with this writing. My dear departed father Elder Willie Schofield Sr., in whose household and churches I was reared in as a child. My father introduced the apostolic way to the Schofield family and went on to pastor two churches that are still thriving even after his demise. To my current pastor and mother the venerable Dr. Tanner Schofield Cole who has been my pastor for most of my 27 years in the Lord. Pastor Tanner has been my mentor, teacher, and instructor in things pertaining to this Great God we call Jesus. To the Calvary church family, to my daughter Stephanie who has never given her father any trouble and has been saved over half of her life. To my son Richard II whom I have never had to go to court or the jail house to retrieve him, he likewise has been saved for over half of his life. Now I have saved the best for last, my lovely and talented wife "Rometta." When I met Rometta she had already been saved for about ten years. We met in May of 1979, I was saved in October of the same year, and we married in February 1980. I gave you that little history on us so you can appreciate what Rometta had to go through with. She was somewhat seasoned with Christ and I was a new convert. There were many issues in my life that I had to overcome and she stayed with me until God gave me the victory. One of the things I love about my wife is she did not crowd God and try to make me "her" Christian. Rometta allowed God to wire me as he so desired and this writing is a direct result of a wife loving her husband and letting God go to work on him.

Who's on Fire?

I would like you to consider Daniel 3:25: "The form of the fourth is like the Son of God." I am sure you know the story of Shadrach, Meshach, and Abednego and how they were cast into a fiery furnace that was heated seven times hotter because they would not fall down and worship the image (false god). However, after casting in the three men, King Nebuchadnezzar said, "I see four men loose . . . the form of the fourth is like the Son of God" (verse 25). After Jesus rescued Peter from walking on the water in Matthew 14:33, those in the ship said, "Of a truth thou art the Son of God." The devils, who were once heavenly beings (Revelation 12:9), declare in Luke 4:41, "Thou art Christ the Son of God." The Ethiopian eunuch whom Philip ministered to in Acts 8:30 was reading Isaiah 53:7: "He was led as a sheep to the slaughter; and like a lamb dumb before his shearer, so opened he not his mouth." In Acts 8:34 the eunuch wanted to know who this was written about and Philip begun at that scripture and preached to him Jesus. When the eunuch became convicted and wanted to be baptized, Philip said, "If thou believeth with all thine heart." The eunuch said, "I believe that Jesus Christ is the Son of God." Philip, one of the original twelve apostles, one who walked with Jesus, did not rebuke or correct this statement because Jesus *is* the Son of God. If Jesus is the Son of God, who did the king see in the fiery furnace?

As you read this book, I want you to keep one word in the forefront of your mind, the word is *access*. God has access to anything, anyone, anytime, anywhere, anyway He so chooses. Jeremiah 1:5 declares, "Before I formed thee in the belly I knew thee." He had access to Jeremiah before Jeremiah was in his mother's womb. What a mighty God.

Consider John 4:24—God is a spirit. Consider Colossians 1:13—who (speaking of Jesus) is the image of the invisible God. Look at Genesis 1:26—and God said let us make man in our image, after our likeness. This is where many churchgoers get more than one God. Have you ever seen a spirit? Have you ever seen the invisible? What image or likeness does a spirit have, especially if you can't see it to make that determination? Remember the word access. Hebrews 1:2-3 declares, "Hath in these last days spoken unto us by his Son [Jesus], whom he hath appointed heir of all things, by whom also he made the worlds, who being the brightness of his glory and the express image of his person." Yes, Jesus is the express image of God, so who was there during creation? John 1:3: "All things were made by him and without him was not anything made that was made." We must understand that this verse is speaking of the Word. When we look at verse 14 in this chapter we find the Word was made flesh. When I understand this with the help of the Holy Ghost, I find that the Word was something else before becoming flesh, because it had to be made flesh. When the Word was made flesh, that flesh was Jesus Christ, because verse 14 says "and dwelt among us and we beheld his glory. The glory as of the only begotten of the father." Jesus Christ was the only begotten Son of God. Since a spirit does not cast an image, the only image present was Jesus Christ who became the model from which man was made. We must remember that without Jesus Christ was not anything made that was made. If it was made, Jesus made it.

In Isaiah 9, the name Isaiah means Salvation of Jehovah. Some preachers call him the eagle-eye prophet because God allowed him to see far into the future and see the day of salvation. However, before he was called a prophet he was called a seer, according to 1 Samuel 9:9: "He that is now called a prophet was before time called a seer." One of the many things God allowed Isaiah to see and record is in Isaiah 9:6, "Unto us a child is born, unto us a son is given." Look closely at what God showed Isaiah about this child: His name shall be called [notice the word *name* is singular] wonderful counselor, the mighty God, the everlasting Father, the Prince of Peace." Please think of all the prophets, seers, apostles, and angels who even came close to the exploits of Jesus Christ while He was on earth. Isaiah called this child the mighty God, how can we who are filled with the Holy Ghost not see who Jesus really is? David, in Psalm 139:14, got the revelation about how he was put together and said, "I am fearfully and wonderfully made." He is saying he is an awesome wonder, because he was made in His image and likeness, which explains the greatness of God. We are intelligent, inventors, scholars, and great athletes. Our doctors can open a body, a body they had absolutely no part in its design, and cause some functions to operate as they should. If we are as awesome as we are, surely our creator is greater than the creation.

Look at Isaiah 46:9: "I am God, and there is none else, I am God and there is none like me." This clearly tells us Jesus is not a separate entity from God, but is the almighty God. Remember Isaiah 9:6, "his name shall be called . . . the mighty God." Jesus is not *like* God, He *is* God. You are not like yourself, you are yourself.

He is the mighty God (Isaiah 46:10) declaring the end from the beginning. To declare means to make known. With that in mind, the word access comes up again. God has access to everything because there are no boundaries to Him. Consider John 20:19, "When the doors were shut where the disciples were assembled for fear of the Jews, Jesus came and stood in their midst." The Scripture plainly tells us they were in fear and the doors were shut—so our God just simply walked through the wall. Physically speaking, no boundaries can contain him. His tomb couldn't hold him. He called Lazarus (John 11:43) from beyond the grave; he heard Him and responded to His voice. Time is no boundary to him. In John 8:56-58 Jesus said, "Your father Abraham rejoiced to see my day and he saw it and was glad [compare Genesis 18:2-3] and he lifted up his eye and looked, and, lo, three men stood by him: and when he saw them, he ran to meet them from the tent door, and bowed himself toward the ground, and said, 'My Lord, if now I have found favor in thy sight, pass not away, I pray thee, from thy servant.'" John 8:57 declares, "Thou art not yet fifty years old, and hast thou seen Abraham?" Jesus continued in verse 58: "Verily, verily I say unto you, before Abraham was, I am." Just as they attempted to stone Him then, rocks are still being thrown today when one dares to declare Jesus is God. The law of buoyancy was abused in Matthew 14:25 when Jesus walked on the sea. He made a mockery of the law of gravity in Acts 1:9 when He was taken up and a cloud received Him (talking about Hang Time) out of their sight. The point? Nothing can hinder our God from doing what He wants to do. It is possible for Him to have access to His body at any time, before or after Mary the mother of Jesus. There are no barriers to our God. Hebrews 1:2: "Hath in these last days spoken unto us by his Son [Jesus] whom he hath appointed heir of all things, by whom [Jesus] also he made the worlds." Hebrews 13:8 says, "Jesus Christ the same yesterday, today and forever." These scriptures declare Jesus as eternal; how else can something or someone not change except it be eternal?

Jesus does not evolve. John 17:24 declares that God loved Him before the foundation of the world. I am aware that some will say Jesus was just a thought in the mind of God; what kind of a thought can create worlds as we see in Hebrews 1:2? Thoughts do not create, thinkers create. Examine Genesis 18:10-11: "Sarah thy wife shall have a son . . . Abraham and Sarah were old and well stricken in age [he was ninety-nine]." They were so old and past childbearing years that Sarah laughed (verse 12) at such a promise, but the Lord said in verse 14, "Is anything too hard for the Lord?" You and I will never see with our natural eye or understand with our natural mind how Jesus can present himself as a man in the Old Testament and come to us as a baby (Matthew 1:23 — Emmanuel, God with us) in the New Testament. He put Himself in the womb of a virgin (Matthew 1:23). Science could use artificial insemination, but I am so glad God used Spirit insemination (Luke 1:35). Since He remains the same (Hebrews 13:8), as I grow in Christ and find out how great He really is, I must remember whatever I discover about Him ten years from how, He is that right now. Right now I believe He is a healer, but I won't know it until He heals my body. When God saved me on October 11, 1979, even though I was raised in an apostolic family, I still had to believe who Jesus was. I had to learn to allow the Spirit to reveal to me who I was serving. Matthew 11:29 says, "Take my yoke upon you, and learn of me." Brothers and sisters, we all must learn who Jesus really is.

New Testament

Look at Luke 1:28. "The angel came to her and said, 'Hail thou that art highly favored.'" Verse 31, "Thou shalt conceive in thy womb and bring forth a son and shalt call his name Jesus." Verse 34: "How shall this be, seeing I know not a man?" There seems to be some skepticism on Mary's part, as with Sarah. I am sure if we lived in those days, we too would have had some questions concerning a ninety-year-old woman (Genesis 18:10) and a virgin (Luke 1:34) giving birth. This led Gabriel the angel in Luke 1 to say in verse 37, "With God nothing shall be impossible." I truly hope we can remove the limits our lack of faith imposes on our growth in God.

I would like us to understand that if God can make a path of dry ground through the Red Sea (Exodus 14:21), form dirt to look like the image of God (Genesis 1:26), and breathe into man's nostrils so he became a living soul (Genesis 2:7)—if you can believe God did all that and a whole lot more—why can't He present himself as a baby who will become the sacrifice for our sins? I remind us of the word access which simply means the capacity to enter or approach. God can and does enter into any dimension, any dispensation, any time, in any period of history, anywhere He chooses to apply to Himself. What doctor did He consult when He removed a rib from Adam's side and closed his flesh instead thereof (Genesis 2:21)? What group of scientists did He brainstorm with when He created the universe? What zoo did He seek advice from when He designed the animals, what agriculturist told Him what seeds should be planted?

Galatians 4:4 speaks on this: "When the fullness of time was come, God sent forth his Son, made of a woman [Mary], made under the law." He chose to be governed by earthly laws to some extent (more on this later). Notice what Galatians 4:4 states, "God sent forth his son." Compare this with John 12:44-45 where Jesus said, "He that believeth on me, believeth not on me, but on him who sent me . . . and he that seeth me seeth him who sent me." I understand You very well Jesus: when I see You, I see God because You were big enough to send Yourself.

I present this scenario. John is married to Susie. John gets home after work but Susie is still at work. John exercises about five or six times a week. This particular day, after a hard day at work, John is sitting in his Lazyboy and contemplating not doing his workout. His wife is not there to encourage him so he just sits and thinks about not going. However, as he is thinking about not going, the benefits he has already received from working out come to his mind.

After twenty minutes he decides to get his session started. When John enters the gym he is spotted by a co-worker who promptly says, "I know you had a hard day at work and didn't feel like working out. I guess Susie sent you to do your workout." John tells him, "No, I sent myself." My point? Why can't we just allow God to govern Himself as He governs us? He seems to be doing a great job.

When we look at Luke 2:52—Jesus increased in wisdom and statue—some think that if Jesus is God, how can He increase in wisdom? Is not God all knowing? When the Bible speaks of Jesus, the flesh of God, remember in 1 Timothy 3:16 that God was manifest in the flesh. Manifest simply means to make visible, since God is a spirit.

Colossians 1:15 says the image of the invisible God; He simply put on some clothes (flesh) so we could see Him. Sometimes, when a married couple has a baby, the clothes don't always fit as well as they should. Shirts are too large, shoes are too long, and the pants are too long. The parents say he will grow into them. It's like that with God being Jesus—but the opposite. In this case, the clothes have to grow to fit the spirit. Remember, we have a child whose father is a spirit (Luke 1:35) and who was born to a virgin. What an entrance our God made into this world, and His bodily exit was just as spectacular. We must remember our God has access to anything that can assist Him to bring about His master plan of salvation. He created life, so He can tweak it, He can roll it back, He can roll it forward, sideways, up or down, or whatever pleases Him to get His will done. Deuteronomy 4:35 declares, "The Lord he is God; there is none else beside him." He does not have to call a meeting when He gets ready to do something. He is the committee, the judge, jury, and executioner.

It's All in the Family

Remember what I said in the introduction, the content of this book is meant for Spirit-filled believers who have not so much as heard that Jesus is God. I have no problem with others reading these pages; however, Scripture says no one can say Jesus is Lord, except by the Holy Ghost. John 10:30: "I and my father are one." Some scriptures do not require a great deal of interpretation, exegesis, or brow beating to understand. For example, "Jesus wept" (John 11:35). The disciples saw Him walking on the sea in Matthew 14:26. In John 11:43-44, Jesus cried with a loud voice, "Lazarus come forth" and he did. These verses do not require you to go on a fast, get six or seven Bible-related books, and study for weeks to get an understanding; they are straightforward. They say what they mean and mean what they say. John 10:30 is one of those scriptures. Translated, it simply means God and Jesus are the same. I am a father, husband, and son; I can truthfully say I and my children's father are one. I and my wife's husband are one. I and my mother's son are one. Why can't Jesus and God be one? Allow me to speak this into your spirit: 1 Timothy 3:16, "And without controversy great is the mystery of godliness: God was manifest in the flesh, justified in the Spirit, seen of angels, preached unto the Gentiles, believed on in the world, received up into glory." This verse is to Spirit-filled believers because it is speaking of God being manifested in the flesh, so remember, only Spirit-filled people can say with authority that Jesus is God.

The word controversy means a clash of opposing views or to dispute. Those of us who have the Holy Ghost have the selfsame Spirit according to 1 Corinthians 12:11, "All these [diversities of gifts, 1 Corinthians 12:4] worketh that one and the selfsame spirit, dividing to every man severally as he will." If we have the same Holy Ghost even though none of us speak or sound alike, we know it's the Holy Ghost when we hear him. That is God's unique way of letting us know we have the same Holy Ghost and that we are of the same family. We must recognize that God has but one Spirit and that is what the Holy Ghost is, the spirit of God, according to John 15:26, "But when the Comforter [the Holy Ghost, John 14:26] is come, who I will send unto you from the Father even the Spirit of truth, which proceedeth from the Father, he shall testify of me." Look at it this way: we have a spirit coming from the Father that will testify about Jesus, because Jesus has been talking in this passage ever since verse 19 in the sixteenth chapter, continuing on over into the seventeenth chapter. There is no division in Christ. James 1:17 declares,

"With whom is no variableness, neither shadow of turning." God wants us who are filled with His Spirit to believe the same thing. A family resembles one another—they sound alike, they look alike, and they surely agree on who their father is. I suppose some Spirit-filled believers have pastors who have not come to the revelation, so this makes it hard for those of you who really have a thirst to know what is really going on. Jeremiah 23:1 states, "Woe be unto the pastors that destroy and scatter the sheep of my pasture; saith the Lord." To those of you who are still under those pastors who believe Jesus and God are two separate gods, I quote Philippians 2:12, "Work out your own salvation with fear and trembling." John 8:24 screams at us and declares, "If ye believe not that I am he, ye shall die in your sins." Did you know it is a sin not to believe Jesus is God? Verse 27 says, "They understood not that he spake to them of the Father."

First Timothy 3:16: "Great is the mystery of godliness." Mystery here means a religious truth known by revelation alone. Faith is the key to unlock mysteries. Hebrews 11:1: "Faith is the substance of things hoped for, the evidence of things not seen." You can have evidence of something you can't see. Believers, allow me to help you see something about yourself that you may not have thought about. I am talking to those of you who have the Holy Ghost according to Acts 2:4, "And they were all filled with the Holy Ghost, and began to speak with other tongues as the Spirit gave them utterance." Consider the amount of faith you exercised to receive the Holy

Ghost: first you had to believe in a God you had never seen, you had to believe you would speak a language you never learned in school, and now you are believing this God you have never seen will one day soon split the sky and rapture you up, without the aid of a spacecraft, to a place you have never been or seen—and yet you have a problem believing that Jesus is the almighty God? Jesus is God. He is not God because I say so, it is simply because Jesus is God. The revelation is a dayspring in my soul and the Scriptures bear it out. That's what gives me the conviction to write this revelation.

Doubting Thomas

I suppose we should have doubters today, because Christ had to deal with them in His cabinet. Thomas, one of the twelve apostles, doubted the resurrection of Jesus (John 20:25: "Except I shall see in his hands the print of the nails and put my finger into the print of the nails and thrust (more on thrust in a minute) my hand into his side, I will not believe"). Thomas had seen Jesus on the cross. He doubted any man could come back from such a horrible death, even though he had witnessed Jesus' miracles. It is like we do when faced with a new test or trials. We forget how God took us through other fiery trials. You may face new dilemmas and different situations, but none of these things are new to God. He declared the end from the beginning, He already knows what will befall us. Verse 26 continues, "After eight days again his disciples were within and Thomas with them: then came Jesus, the doors being shut [the reason the Bible says "the doors being shut" is to let us know His entry into the room was not through an open door. Remember, there are no barriers to our God] and stood in the midst and said peace be unto you." In verse 27 Jesus said to Thomas, "Reach hither thy finger and behold my hands; and reach hither thy hand and thrust it into my side." The word *thrust* means to drive with force, stab, or pierce. Thomas literally put his hand inside the wound left by the spear the soldier used to pierce our Lord's side (John 19:34). While Thomas still had his hand in our Lord's side, the Lord downloaded into Thomas's spirit who He really was, thus the words that fell from Thomas's lips: "My Lord and my God" (verse 28).

Pay close attention to whom Thomas is talking. He is talking to Jesus Christ and he calls Him "my Lord and my God." Do you see it yet? Sometimes doubt can be used in a positive way. Thomas's doubt caused him to seek a more infallible proof of the risen Lord. We doubt things we are unaware of or have never been informed about. Jeremiah 6:16: "Thus saith the Lord, stand ye in the ways, and see, and ask for the old paths where is the good way and walk therein and ye shall find rest for your souls." I think it may be like a son searching for the father he has never known. God does not want to be unknown to His children, He wants to foster a relationship with the children for whom He laid down his life. John 10:10: "The thief [the devil] cometh not, but for to steal and to kill and to destroy; I [Jesus] am come that they [us] might have life and that they might have it more abundantly." The enemy would love for you not to know who your father is. If you don't, you won't know who to call when trouble is all around you. Matthew 7:22-23: "Many will say to me in that day, Lord, Lord have we not prophesied in thy name? And in thy name have cast out devils? And in thy name done many wonderful works? And then will I profess unto them, I never knew [been intimate with] you: depart from me, ye that work iniquity [wickedness]." We do not want to hear those words from our Lord just because we did not try to find out who He really is.

The Road to Damascus

A tentmaker by trade and a student of Gamaliel, a prolific teacher of the law, Saul began his persecution of the church. Saul is first mentioned at the stoning of Stephen in Acts 7:58: "The witnesses laid down their clothes at a young man's feet, whose name was Saul." In Acts 8:3 we see Saul making havoc of the church, entering into every house and dragging, pulling, or pushing men and women, committing them to prison. Saul was determined to stop everyone he heard calling on the name of Jesus. In Acts 9:1 Saul was "yet breathing out threatenings and slaughter against the disciples of the Lord." The word *slaughter* indicates butchery, massacre, or overkill; there seems to be more to it than mere execution. Saul was overtaken with anger, not only at the name of Jesus, but because the disciples believed in Jesus as the Messiah. Saul went to the synagogues in Damascus looking for people who were of "this way" [of this religion] (Acts 9:2) so he could arrest and bring them bound to Jerusalem. What hatred Saul had for the Christians who only wanted to worship and praise God. The Bible is indeed a bloody book—blood in the Old Testament, blood on the cross, and blood after the cross. While on his journey to persecute the Christians, God posted a stop sign on the road to Damascus. I believe the saints had prayed to God about Saul and wondered when God would stop this enemy of the church. Ananias, in chapter 9:13, said, "I have heard by many of this man, how much evil he hath done to thy saints at Jerusalem . . . to bind all that call on thy name." Acts 9:3: "Suddenly there shined round about him a light from heaven." Paul describes it in Acts 26:13: "I saw in the way a light from heaven above the brightness of the sun." How long can you stare at the sun? Maybe a few seconds. Imagine a light above the brightness of the sun! Saul was in trouble and he knew it. Acts 9:4: "Saul, Saul why persecutest thou me?" I suppose the light and the voice gave some identity to Saul as to whom he was dealing with. Saul, when he bound some old mother or father and brought them to court to face a stoning, probably did not consider he was persecuting God. Matthew 25:40: "Inasmuch as ye have done unto one of the least of these my brethren, ye have done it unto me."

What I want us to understand is whatever we do to God's saints, be it good or bad, we do it to Him. It's like a bully beating up on your sister; he might as well have hit you. It may seem like God has forgotten your pleas, but I assure you He will never leave nor forsake you. God deals in the fullness of time; He can see the end from the beginning and knows the best time for deliverance. Saul's reply in Acts 9:5—who art thou Lord? Remember that Saul is well-educated and knows the word *Lord* is not a name but a title, a title meaning absolute control. Our Lord accepts the occasion to identify Himself. Pay close attention to these next few words. In verse; 5 "And the Lord said, 'I am Jesus whom thou persecutest.'" The one who is in absolute control said *I am Jesus*. If the Lord identifies Himself as Jesus, it looks like case closed. Jesus really is God. In Acts 9:4 Saul fell to the earth when he heard the voice saying, "Saul, Saul, why persecutest thou me?" There was no committee, no more than one voice speaking. Colossians 2:9 says in Christ dwells all the fullness of the Godhead bodily.

I must address something else that was taking place on the road to Damascus. Saul was not aware of it at the time, but this was the beginning of his apostleship. Saul's account of what happened on the road is recorded in Acts 26:16: "Rise [Jesus talking] and stand upon thy feet: for I have appeared unto thee for the purpose, to make thee a minister and a witness both of these things which thou hast seen and of these things in the which I will appear unto thee." I won't say we do not have apostles today, but if we do they must have the qualifications of 1 Corinthians 9:1—"Am I not free? Have I not seen Jesus Christ our Lord? [Notice how he calls Jesus *Lord*]. Are not ye my work in the Lord?" Also, in 2 Corinthians 12:12: "Truly the signs of an apostle were wrought among you in all patience, in signs and wonders, and mighty deeds." We can see how it is possible to be mistaken about something you are really serious about. Paul, in his Acts 22:3 testimony, mentions how he was "zealous toward God, as ye all are this day." Even in his zeal, still thinking he's right, verse 4: "I persecuted this way unto death." It is possible to be mistaken about something, and at the same time think you're right. Maybe that is why God did not kill Saul; He knew he would be converted and become one of the most powerful apostles in the Bible. Saul discovered he could serve God by serving Jesus. He discovered that Jesus and God are one and the same.

Proof that Paul believed Jesus is God can be found in Acts 20:28: "Which the Holy Ghost hath made you overseers, to feed the church of God, which he purchased with his own blood." God and blood in the same sentence sounds like Jesus to me.

Thomas, another of the original twelve, said to Jesus in John 14:5, "How can we know the way?" Listen carefully to our Lord's reply in verse 6: "I am the way, the truth and the life: no man cometh unto the Father, but by me." Verse 7 declares, "If ye had known me, ye should have known my Father also: and from hence forth ye know him and have seen him." I truly hope the Holy Ghost is working to give you the revelation. He says, "If ye had known me." Some of us don't take time to learn who Jesus is. In Matthew 11:29 Jesus says, "Take my yoke upon you and learn of me." We must learn who we have when we take on this Jesus. Jesus told Thomas in John 14:7, "Henceforth ye know him [Jesus] and have seen him, because Jesus is in the Father and the Father is in him." Our Lord told Phillip, another of the twelve, in verse 9, "He who has seen me hath seen the Father." Jesus is all of the Father we shall ever see.

Allow me to paint this picture. My father, the late Elder Willie Schofield Sr., passed away a few years ago. You cannot see him any longer on this earth. I look at his picture sometimes, but it's only an image and does not do his presence justice. However, when I am around my two sisters and four brothers and some of our nieces and nephews, I truly see my father. I see him because his traits—his mannerisms, his preaching style, his voice, and his presence collectively emanate from each of them. When I see my family, I see my father. In John 14:26, Jesus informs us the Holy Ghost will teach us all things. If we allow the Holy Ghost to lead and direct our thoughts and our mind, we will get a better understanding of who Jesus is. I remind you again—it does not matter how eloquently one speaks or writes. If the Holy Ghost does not give the revelation, there will be no revelation. That is why I constantly remind you to lean heavily on the Holy Ghost to reveal the hidden things of God. Consider John 16:13: "When he, the spirit of truth is come, He will guide you into all [not some] truth . . . and will show you things to come."

I AM

In Exodus 3:13 Moses said to God, "When I come unto the children of Israel, and shall say unto them, the God of your fathers hath sent me unto you; and they shall say to me, what is his [God's] name? What shall I say unto them?" In verse 14 God said to Moses, "I AM THAT I AM: and he said, thus shalt thou say unto the children of Israel, I AM hath sent me unto you." Moses recognized the word *God* is not a name. God is an office or a title given to the person or thing that is the occupant. The proof follows in that God did not rebuke Moses for asking for a name; on the contrary, He granted his request and gave him His name. The office of president of the USA must be occupied by someone before the office is effective. Once a person is elected to this office, they are called by the title of the office. Reporters and politicians refer to the person in that office as the president, Mr. President, or the commander in chief. I have watched the president at news conferences; he answers and acknowledges these titles, but that is not his name:

his name is George Bush. I can imagine in Moses' mind he knew God was the creator, his provider, his God, the God of Abraham, Isaac and Jacob but what is the name of this God? Understand that this God has many names, depending on which dimension He is operating in.

Genesis 17:1: "When Abram was ninety years old and nine, the Lord appeared to Abram and said unto him, I am the Almighty God." In John 8:58 Jesus said, "Verily, verily I say unto you, before Abraham was I am." "I am" simply means I am who I am, the absolute I, the self-existent one. To examine the word am, look at the word *be*.

> Be — past first and third person singular: was
> Be — second person singular: were
> Be — past participle: been
> Be — present participle: being
> Be — present first participle: AM

If we put them all together we get I was, I were, I've been, I am being, and I am. Our Lord is omnipresent because He has no beginning of days. The psalmist writes in Psalm 118:24: "This is the day which the Lord hath made." John 1:3 says, "All things were made by him." The day was made by Jesus; therefore, he fills all time and space because it was created by Him. I doubt you could find a Ford automobile without the name or emblem of Ford attached. I know we cannot find a day in all history that does not have the emblem of Jesus on it because

He made all things. I pose some questions to Jesus, the great I am.

> Were you the one who made man from the dust of the ground? *I am.*
>
> Were you the one God spoke to in Genesis, saying, "Let us make man in our image and after our
> likeness? *I was.*
>
> Who was the fourth person in the fiery furnace? *I was.*
>
> Who is the greatest who ever came down from heaven? *I am.*

Some Old Testament scriptures about I Am.
> I am thy shield and thy exceeding great reward (Genesis 15:1).
> I am the Almighty God (Genesis 17:1).
> I am the Lord that healeth thee (Exodus 15:26).
> I am the rose of Sharon and the lily of the valleys (Song of Solomon 2:1).
> I am he (Isaiah 43:25).
> I am the first; I also am the last (Isaiah 48:12).
> I am merciful (Jeremiah 3:12).

Some New Testament scriptures:
> I am the bread of life (John 6:35, 41, 48, 51).
> I am the light of the world (John 8:12).
> I am the door (John 10:7, 9).

I am the good shepherd (John 10:11, 14).
I am the resurrection and the life (John 11:25).
I am the way, the truth, and the life (John 14:6).
I am the true vine (John 15:1, 5).
I am Jesus whom thou persecutest (Acts 9:5).
I am Alpha and Omega (Revelation 1:8).
I am the root and the offspring of David and the bright and morning star. (Revelations 22:16)

Please note that all the above are singular, never plural. Yes, Jesus is the almighty God.

The Word

There are many scriptures that explain who Jesus really is, but my favorite is John 1:1—"In the beginning was the Word, and the Word was with God, and the Word was God." Verse 2 of the same chapter: "The same [the Word] was in the beginning with God." Look closely at verse 14: "And the Word was made flesh and dwelt among us, (and we beheld his glory, the glory as of the only begotten of the Father) full of grace and truth." Look at John 3:16, "For God so loved the world that he gave his only begotten Son." I hope you agree that the *only begotten* in verse 14 is the same *only begotten* in 3:16 because there is only one "only begotten"—Jesus. Verse 14 tells us the Word was made flesh, so we can be sure John is speaking of Jesus, because He is the only begotten son of the Father. If you are still with me, fasten your seatbelts a little tighter as we prepare to takeoff as I insert "Jesus" in the place of "the *word*" in John 1:1-2, simply because "the Word" was given a name and an identity in verse 14. "In the beginning was

Jesus and Jesus was with God and Jesus was God. The same "Jesus" was in the beginning with God." My name is Richard; I am not only with me, I am me. Do you see what the Holy Ghost is showing us? Verse 3 in chapter 1 tells us all things were made by Him. Who is Him? Look at John 1:2: "The same [the Word] was in the beginning with God." So the *Him* is the one who was made flesh, none other than Jesus Christ. I remind us that Jesus has no boundaries and God has access to anything, anyone, anyplace, and anywhere He decides to do His work.

Mount of Transfiguration

The word *transfiguration* means to transform from one form to another. The Greek for transfiguration, μεταμόρφωση, means *metamorphoo* which we recognize today as metamorphoses, a change of physical form and structure by supernatural means. Mark's account of the transfiguration is in chapter 9:2-3—"Jesus taketh with him Peter and James and John and leadeth them up into a high mountain apart by themselves; and he was transfigured before them. His raiment became shining exceeding white as snow: so as no fuller on earth can white them." Jesus was transfigured before their eyes. Peter, James, and John made up Christ's inner circle. Jesus chose twelve but only trusted three to witness the transfiguration. What was Jesus being transfigured to? Remember, transfigured means to be transformed from one form to another.

John, who was present, wrote in John 1:14: "We beheld his glory, the glory as of the only begotten of the Father." I am certain the cloud in Mark 9:7 was there to prevent Peter, James, and John from seeing too much. I say that because of 1 John 3:2—"It doth not yet appear what we shall be: but we know that when He shall appear [come back for us by rapture] we shall be like [look like] him; for we shall see him as he is [in all his glory]." Isn't it exciting to know we will get a new body and leave this old one behind?

The Mystery of Godliness

The word *mystery* in the Bible means "to shut the mouth." The mouth can speak of those things that the mind has knowledge of, but when there is no knowledge the mouth is shut. That is why in the beginning of this book I quoted 1 Corinthians 12:3: "No man can say that Jesus is the Lord, but by the Holy Ghost." Even with the Holy Ghost, God does not reveal everything to His people. First Corinthians 13:12 reminds us that "for now we see through a glass darkly; but then face to face: Now I know in part; but then shall I know even as also I am known." We take what God gives us; what He does not give us we leave alone. The mystery of godliness is revealed in part—the part that is essential to salvation. We must know that Jesus is God. To be saved according to John 8:24: "If ye believe not that I am he [God] ye shall die in your sins." Verse 27: "They understood not that he spoke to them of the Father." In 1 Timothy 3:16 we see, "And without controversy great is the mystery of godliness." I have learned that before any

Spirit-filled person can believe Jesus is God they must first rid themselves of their ideas. Some try to understand how God presented Himself as a grown man in the Old Testament and then came as a baby in the New Testament. Because they cannot, with their natural mind, understand the mystery, they find themselves sitting atop the fence. The Bible tells us we must worship God in spirit and in truth, so we must use that same spirit to know who He is. Human reasoning and intellect (no matter how high your IQ) can never reveal who Jesus is. When Jesus asked His apostles who they believed Him to be, the answer was, "Thou art the Christ, the Son of the living God." Jesus replied in Matthew 16:17, "Flesh and blood hath not revealed it unto thee, but my Father which is in heaven." I am sure, as you should be by now, that the Spirit makes all the revelation of who God is and anything else in the spirit world we need to know.

First Timothy 3:16—"God was manifest in the flesh." The word *manifest* means to make known. The contents of a ship or an eighteen wheeler are listed on its manifest. The manifest tells us what's inside. The common cold germ can enter the body and lie dormant for hours and even days before it manifests itself with symptoms of a cough, runny nose, or sneezing. The understanding I gather from this scripture is that God was made known in the flesh. How exactly was He made known in the flesh? In John 1:14, we saw that the Word was made (known) flesh. We already know that flesh was Christ. If God was manifested in the flesh as Jesus Christ and there remained only one entity, wouldn't that mean God and Jesus are one?

Jesus is God all day long, not because I say so, but because the Bible offers many infallible proofs that Jesus Christ is indeed the almighty God.

Explore the latter clause of 1 Timothy 3:16: "Justified in the spirit, seen of angels, preached unto the Gentiles, believed on in the world, received up into glory." I trust you agree that these things happened to God after He was manifested in the flesh. Who was received into glory? Whoever it was that God became in the flesh. Acts 1:11 tells us, "The same Jesus, which is taken up from you into heaven, shall so come in like manner as ye have seen him go into heaven." Here is more help from John 3:13: "No man hath ascended up to heaven, but he that came down from heaven, even the Son of man which is in heaven." Having said this, it should be clear that if God descended it was God who ascended, because the Scripture declares that the coming down and the going up to glory was done by the same one. If we follow Scripture, we must at some point in our walk with Christ allow the Holy Spirit to give revelation.

Fashioned as a Man

Philippians 2:5-6: "Let this mind be in you which was also in Christ Jesus: who, being in the form of God, thought it not robbery to be equal with God." To explain this I illustrate with my dear mother. My mother, Dr. Tanner Schofield Cole, is also my pastor. Sometimes she speaks to me as my mother and other times it is as my pastor. Let there be no misunderstanding, I am very aware of which form she is using. If it's a family matter, she may choose to speak in the form of my mother; if it's church business she will likely speak as my pastor. Jesus Christ is the form of God. The word *form* is *paniym* (paw-neem) in Hebrew, which means face. Jesus is the face of God. Remember what Jesus said in John 12:45, "He that seeth me seeth Him that sent me." When we look at the latter clause of Philippians 2:6—thought it not robbery—we think of a robber taking something that doesn't belong to him. You cannot steal from yourself. The other word we must look at is *equal*; it means a same measure, a same value. We understand

Jesus thought it not a theft to be the same as God, because He is fully God already. Verse 7 tells us He took upon Him the form (face) of a servant and was made in the likeness of man. God took on the face (form) of a servant (Jesus) and was made in the likeness of men (Jesus). Verse 8 says, "Being found in fashion [to resemble] a man, he humbled himself, laying aside his splendor and magnificence." He who created and gave life was above the domain of death, but for our good, He became submissive unto death. Why? Because, as John 10:18 says, "No man taketh it [life] from me, but I [Jesus] lay it down of myself. I have power to lay it down and I have power to take it again." I ask, "How can Jesus, who was flesh like you and me, die and pick up His life again? How can a man die and live again, even after He was entombed? The answer: no man can, but God can do anything. Try to imagine the power to stop living and start it again, all at your own discretion. What a mighty God we serve!

What Happened on the Cross?

I have heard the argument, that if Jesus was God how could they kill Him on the cross? They never killed him. Remember John 10:18: "No man taketh it [life] from me, but I lay it down . . . and I have power to take it again." John 1 tells us the Word was God and that the Word was made flesh (verse 14). I mentioned before that Jesus was the flesh of God; they crucified that flesh on the cross for your sins and mine. Whenever sin was committed, a sacrifice was required. Jesus was the last and ultimate sacrifice for sin. Second Corinthians 5:21: "For he hath made him to be sin for us, who knew no sin; that we might be made the righteousness of God in Him." That is why the animals that were sacrificed knew no sin. They were not aware sin existed. When Christ became sin for us, He took all our sins upon Himself and became responsible for the debt we owed to get us out of sin. When He cried, "Why hast thou forsaken me?" it was the flesh (Jesus) crying out because He felt the Holy Ghost about to leave him. Luke 9:23: "If any man will come after me, let him deny himself and take up his cross daily and follow me." God in the form of Jesus at Calvary denied Himself so His body could die and complete the sacrifice. Had He not forsaken His body, becoming sin for us, there would have been no death on Calvary. Remember, they could not take His life, He had to lay it down.

Who Was Melchisedec?

Melchisedec simply means king of righteousness and king of Salem (peace). Romans 3:22 says "Righteousness of God, which is by faith of Jesus Christ." If someone is called the king of righteousness and peace, he must be someone who can create righteousness and declare peace. Who can do that other than God? Hebrews 7:3 speaks of Melchisedec — without father, without mother . . . having neither beginning of days nor end of life. Jesus Christ displayed some of these attributes. He was born without an earthly father, and even though He laid down His life for a brief moment, Luke 24:6 declares "He is not here [in the tomb] but is risen," so his days continue even now. My question: who can come into being without a mother or father and have no end to their days? In Hebrews 7:14, it is evident that Jesus Christ sprang out of Judea; of which tribe Moses spoke nothing concerning priesthood (verse 15). "And it is yet far more evident: for that after the similitude of Melchisedec there ariseth another priest." Verse 16: "Who is made not after the law of a carnal commandment, but after the power of an endless life." In Hebrews 7:3 we read, "But made like unto the Son of God; abideth a priest continually [speaking of Melchisedec]." We look at Hebrews 5:6: "Thou art a priest for ever after the order of Melchisedec [speaking of Christ]." We have two who have no end to their life, two who are declared a high priest forever—one who is declared to be after the order of the other. Maybe they are one and the same—do you think we will see two high priests in heaven? Hebrews 4:15: "We have not an high priest [singular] which cannot be touched with the feeling of our infirmities." Remember, God has access. Hebrews 13:8 declares, "Jesus Christ the same yesterday, today, and for ever." How could Jesus possibly know that, unless He had access to each dimension of time— past, present, and future? God alone can reach out of eternity into each of these dimensions and intermingle its events and inhabitants as it pleases Him.

Hebrews 5:7 says, "Who in the days of his flesh." We don't want to get confused and think this verse is speaking of Melchisedec and not Jesus Christ. Earlier I mentioned it was possible that Jesus and Melchisedec were likely the same. I stick with that; just in two different time dimensions. Verse 7 is speaking of Jesus because it says He had offered up prayers and supplications with strong crying and tears to Him who was able to save Him from death. Melchisedec had no beginning or end of days. But Jesus Christ laid down His life. My real concern in this verse is in the days of His flesh. I don't know about you, but that smacks of incarnation. This tells us Jesus was not always flesh. If you are not flesh, that only leaves spirit. He took on flesh to save mankind by laying down his life on Calvary. We sinners needed salvation. God was intent on making expiation for the sins of the world. To make amends for sin, suffering and death was an important part of reconciliation. God became flesh so the flesh, Jesus, could suffer and lay down His life to give mankind a way out of sin. When I became a husband I was still Richard; when I became a father, I was still Richard. God became flesh but never stopped being God.

The Godhead: What Is It?

The word *Godhead* means the nature, attributes, and power of God. Colossians 2:9, "For in him [Christ] dwelleth all the fullness of the Godhead bodily." I like the word bodily as opposed to typically or figuratively. I understand this to mean that God expressed Himself in the flesh; He took on flesh in the person of Jesus Christ, which brings us to the subject of this narrative, God A.K.A, Jesus Christ. We have to understand that whatever God is, however powerful or knowledgeable, all these attributes dwell in Christ Jesus. It is ironic that the Bible often refers to Jesus as the Lord Jesus Christ or, as in Colossians 2:6, Christ Jesus the Lord. When I look up God and Lord in *Unger's Bible Dictionary* they mean the same thing—Yahweh. We know Yahweh means "He causes to be or exist, or He creates." I am convinced by what I read in Scripture that the Lord Jesus Christ simply means the God Jesus Christ. I am convinced Christ Jesus the Lord means Christ Jesus the God. I had the pleasure to talk with Bishop Edward Roberts of Charlotte, NC about this manuscript. In his quiet manner he informed me that Jesus Christ was not in the Godhead, but rather, according to Colossians 2:9, in Jesus Christ dwells all the fullness of the Godhead bodily. Since the Godhead was in Jesus, all the power, attributes, nature, and properties were dwelling in His being. This is why we call him the Lord (God) Jesus Christ. Matthew 12:34 says, "Out of the abundance of the heart the mouth speaketh." Philip, in John 14:8 said to Jesus, "Lord, show us the father, and it sufficeth [satisfy] us." Jesus' reply came out of the abundance, the fullness of His heart and mind (verse 9): "Have I been so long with you and yet hast thou not known me, Philip? He that hath seen me hath seen the father." Seeing Jesus as God is like looking at the forest and asking, "Where are the trees?" If one must see a tree they must move closer and focus on one tree to get the true meaning of what is before them. When Jesus asked Philip, "Have I been so long time with you and thou hast not known me?" I believe He is asking the same question today. We can be around a person and not know them inwardly. To know who Jesus really is, you must have a relationship that goes beyond Him just being your provider. You must also be filled with the Holy Ghost. According to John 16:13, the Spirit will guide you into all truth and will show you things to come. This is why He spoke as He did, because He is both God and man in one — Jesus Christ the Lord God.

Alpha and Omega

את

Revelation starts this way: "The Revelation of Jesus Christ." The word *revelation* means disclosure, to expose to view, to make known or public. With this meaning in mind, there must be something about Jesus Christ that everyone is unaware of. I affectionately call this book, or at least part of it, the "resume of Jesus Christ." It tells us a lot about Jesus—who He is, where He came from, where He is going, and what He will do last. John speaks in Revelation 1:9, saying he was on the Isle of Patmos "for the word of God, and for the testimony of Jesus Christ." In 1:8 and 11 the introduction God gives to John says, "I am Alpha and Omega . . . the beginning and the ending . . . which is and which was and which is to come, the almighty." Do you remember the "I AM" synopsis—I was, I were, I've been, I am being, I AM. This sounds like He has been here all the time. Do you suppose this is the same Lord who spoke to Saul on the road to Damascus and introduced Himself as Jesus? I do! When we look at Revelation 1:13-16 we get a picture of what to expect when we finally see God. Verse 17: "When I saw him, I fell at his feet as dead: And he laid his right hand upon me, saying unto me, fear not; I am the first and the last." In Revelations 1:8 He identified Himself by the word "*which*." "*Which is*" means present, "*which was*" means the past, and "*which is to come*" means the future.

No other god (notice the lower case "g") can transcend time and space as did the God Jesus Christ. We must pay close attention to how He introduced Himself at the end of verse 8: the Alpha and Omega calls Himself the Almighty. The Greek means *Shadday*, almighty God. It is important to understand that Alpha and Omega means nothing other than God Himself. Look at verse 17 where John says, "When I saw him I fell at his feet as dead." John said he saw Him; the Him he saw was the Alpha and Omega, the first and the last. The first what? To answer that, go to Genesis 1 to see who was the first mentioned in Scripture. Genesis 1:1: "In the beginning God created." This was the beginning of time; eternity has no beginning or end. So Alpha and Omega is telling John He was the first of everything and the last of anything to come. We understand if Alpha and Omega was the beginning and the end, the first and the last, He must be God, the one who was in the beginning. Look at the startling statement of fact He gives to John in Revelation 1:18: "I am he that liveth, and was dead." Wait a minute—Alpha and Omega was at one time dead. Who do we know who was dead, rose, and ascended into heaven? Acts 1:11 tells us it was Jesus, who was taken up into heaven, and will come in like manner "as you have seen him go into heaven." Since Jesus is the only one who was dead, and who rose and ascended into heaven, Alpha and Omega and Jesus must be one and the same. To make this more understandable I put it this way: "God, also known as Jesus Christ." John said in verse 17, "When I saw him [singular]." John saw but one person—Alpha and Omega, who identified Himself in the person of Jesus Christ.

Who Sits on the Throne?

Will you agree with me that He who sits on the throne is God and God alone? In Isaiah 42:8, the Lord says, "I am the Lord: that is my name: and my glory will I not give to another." I am convinced that God is speaking of His name and all the essence and characteristics that go with His name. I have heard some say, "There is power in that name." If we use the Holy Ghost to lead us into all truth, we must come to know God is saying that no other will ever be able to do what He can do. We must understand that of all God will give us, He will never give us the glory to do everything He can. I am sure we will do greater works on this earth than He did, but we will never be God, just sons of God. My point? God will allow no one but Himself to have the glory of sitting on His throne. God took John into heaven and gave him a glimpse of who sits on the throne. We are about to journey into the Scripture of what John saw in heaven. I trust we will agree that He who sits on the throne is God.

Our first stop on this journey is Revelation 4:2: "And immediately I was in the spirit: and behold, a throne was set in heaven, and one sat on the throne." John saw only one on the throne. We must conclude that only one occupies the throne, not two or three. According to verse 9, "Those beasts give glory and honor and thanks to him that sat on the throne, who liveth for ever and ever." We have five witnesses that there is only one on the throne—John and these four beasts. Look at 4:10-11: "The four and twenty elders fall down before him that sat on the throne, and worship him . . . the four and twenty elders say thou art worthy, O Lord to receive glory and honor and power." This verse takes me back to Saul on the road to Damascus. The four and twenty elders call him who sat on the throne Lord. Saul on the road to Damascus had an experience with a light brighter than the sun. Saul called him Lord, and the Lord identified Himself as Jesus. A question: do you feel the Lord on the road to Damascus and the Lord who sat on the throne are the same? I believe they are and I believe the Lord is Jesus Christ. We must continue in verse 11 where the four and twenty elders are speaking: "For thou hast created all things and for thy pleasure they are and were created." I hope you are still in agreement with me, agreeing that the one on the throne is God. The elders called him Lord and said He created all things. Think back to Colossians 1:12-13 where it says, "Giving thanks unto the father, which hath made us meet to be partakers of the inheritance of the saints in light . . . who hath delivered us from the power of darkness and hath translated us into the kingdom of his dear Son [Jesus]." Verse 15-16: "Who is the image of the invisible God, the firstborn of every creature. For by him [the Son, Jesus] were all things created, that are in heaven and that are in earth, visible and invisible. Whether they be thrones or dominions or principalities or powers: all things were created by him [Jesus] and for him." I must stop and examine some of what Paul wrote. Notice verse 16: "By him were all things created." *Him* is singular, meaning one. All things were created by one, Jesus. In the latter clause of verse 16 Paul says, "All things were created by him" [Jesus]. Consider Revelation 4:11: "Thou art worthy, O Lord . . . thou hast created all things." If two different entities were creating all things, it would read *they*. Here is the question: If Jesus created all things in heaven and in earth and in Revelation 4:11 all things were created by "O Lord," are they the same? Both names are singular and there is only one creator, God Almighty, also known as Jesus Christ. John continues his revelation in chapter 5, telling us of the book in the hand of Him who sat on the throne. Verse 5:4: "I wept much, because no man was found worthy to open the book." Thanks be to God for verse 6: "In the midst of the throne and of the four beasts and in the midst of the elders stood a lamb as it had been slain, having seven horns and seven eyes, which are the seven spirits of God sent forth into all the earth." Let us not become confused with the lamb, thinking this is Jesus Christ. I will be the first to say the lamb is symbolic of Jesus Christ. I say symbolic because John named what he saw: a lamb with seven horns and seven eyes, not a man.

Philippians 2:8 says, "Being found in fashion as a man"—speaking of Jesus Christ. Christ as a man had two eyes and no horns. Having said that, the lamb John saw is a tremendous symbol of Jesus Christ being given all power in heaven and on earth. The lamb in Revelation 5:7 took the book out of the right hand of Him who sat on the throne. As we continue in verse 8 we find the four beasts and four and twenty elders fell down before the lamb. I am sure there are not two different worshippings going on in heaven. I bring to your attention Matthew 6:24, "No man can serve two masters: for either he will hate the one and love the other; or else he will hold to the one and despise the other." I think Revelation 17:14 will clear up our minds—"These shall make war with the lamb, and the lamb shall overcome them: for he is Lord of lords and King of kings." What we have here is a mystery taking place in heaven; the result is a symbolic Jesus taking the book out of His own hand, because the elders fell down and worshiped the one who sat on the throne and the lamb. They are the same. We continue this scenario in 20:6—"Blessed and holy is he that hath part in the first resurrection: on such the second death hath no power, but they shall be priests of God and of Christ and shall reign with him a thousand years." Some of you may say this verse has both God and Christ, so the two of them must reign together in heaven. Just reading it as you see it, I can understand how one might get the understanding that two different entities are mentioned. Look closely at exactly what is said after God and Christ are named. I recap this verse with understanding: "But they shall be priest of God and of Christ and shall reign with him [not them] a thousand years." Hopefully, we understand that John mentioned God and Christ but he referred to God and Christ as *Him* not *them*.

I hope we understand that there is no code to understanding God's Word; one cannot dissect this book, figure out some code, and surmise what God is saying. There is no need for anyone to think they can understand the Holy Scriptures without the aid of the Holy Ghost. Paul recounts in Acts 22:3 how he was brought up in Tarsus at the feet of Gamaliel. The biography of Gamaliel says he was such a celebrated doctor of the law, he was one of only seven among the Jewish doctors to be honored with the title of Rabban. He was called the Beauty of the Law. Paul learned at this man's feet; however, in Philippians 3:8 Paul says, "I count all things but loss for the excellency of the knowledge of Christ Jesus my Lord." Education in this world is essential to provide a good quality of life for our families; however, when it comes to the Holy Scriptures and the kingdom of God, one needs the Holy Ghost. Concerning that, I quote James 1:5: "If any of you lack wisdom, let him ask God that giveth to all men liberally and upbraideth not; and it shall be given him." Consider 2 Timothy 2:15, "Study to show thyself approved unto God [not men], a workman that needeth not to be ashamed, rightly dividing the word of truth." We must look at what the word *dividing* means—quite simply, it means separation. You may say, separate what? We must separate what we think from what God is really saying; we can only do that by the indwelling of the

Holy Ghost. Also consider John 16:13, "Howbeit when he, the spirit of truth [the Holy Ghost] is come, he will guide you into all truth: for he [Holy Ghost] shall not speak of himself: But whatsoever he shall hear from the father, that shall he speak: and he [the Holy Ghost] will show you things to come." Second Peter 1:21: "For prophecy came not in old time by the will of man: but holy men of God spoke as they were moved by the Holy Ghost." I say all of that to say this: the Bible had a ghostwriter, the Holy Ghost, so if one will try to understand this book without the aid of the Holy Ghost I take you back to 2 Timothy 2:16-18: "Shun profane and vain babblings: for they will increase unto more ungodliness . . . their word will eat as doth a canker: of whom is Hymenaeus and Philetus . . . who concerning the truth have erred saying that the resurrection is past already: and overthrow the faith of some."

That Rock Was Christ

I am acutely aware that some have a problem with any mention of Jesus Christ in the Old Testament. We must realize He is only mentioned, not revealed, because He said, "Before Abraham was, I am." We must visit 1 Corinthians 10:4: "For they drank of the spiritual Rock that followed them: and that Rock was Christ." The Rock was called spiritual because it gave its water by miraculous and spiritual intervention. We first read about this rock in Exodus 17:6, "Behold I will stand before thee upon the rock in Horeb: and thou shalt smite the rock and there shall come water out of it that the people may drink." My attention goes to the rock in Horeb; it seems Moses and God had a familiarity with this rock. The smiting of this rock was symbolic of the crucifixion of Jesus Christ. We come on this rock a second time in Numbers 20:8, 11: "Take the rod and gather thou the assembly together, thou, and Aaron thy brother and speak ye unto the rock before their eyes; and it shall give forth water, and thou salt bring forth to them water out of the rock . . . and Moses lifted up his hand and with his rod he smote the rock twice: and the water came out abundantly." When we read these passages, we find that Moses in his anger did not do as God had instructed. God said, "Speak to the rock" but Moses hit it twice, symbolizing crucifying Christ. Christ came to die once, for all, and all at once, not every time someone falls in sin. Because Moses did not obey God's directions, God said in Numbers 20:12, "Because ye believed me not to sanctify me in the eyes of the children of Israel, therefore ye shall not bring this congregation into the land which I have given them." Let's go back to the rock in Horeb and the rock in Kadesh. The first time, he hit the rock in Horeb; the second time, he was to speak to the rock, and they were in Kadesh, about 165 miles from Horeb. My question: how did this rock that was big enough for God to stand on in Horeb get to Kadesh 165 miles away? We must go back to 1 Corinthians 10:4: "For they drank of the spiritual Rock that followed them: and that Rock was Christ." Even after God supplied the children of Israel with the necessities of life, they still complained. Look at 1 Corinthians 10:9, "Neither let us tempt Christ, as some of them also tempted and were destroyed of serpents." I hope you see that this verse is saying they tempted Christ during their journey through the wilderness. For a better view, go to the scripture where Paul refers to the Old Testament, Numbers 21:5-6. "And the people spake against God and against Moses, Wherefore have ye brought us up out of Egypt to die in the wilderness? For there is no bread neither is there any water; and our soul loatheth this light bread . . . and the Lord sent fiery serpents among the people and they bit the people; and much people of Israel died." We have to make a determination of where Christ is in this. Verse 5 mentions the people spoke against God and Moses; verse 6 declares the Lord sent fiery serpents. We know Moses is not Christ so that leaves God and the Lord. Remember, 1 Corinthians 10:9 tells us they tempted Christ. If Moses is not Christ, God and the Lord must be Christ. I go back to Numbers 20:8, 10, "Gather thou the assembly together, thou and Aaron thy brother and speak ye unto the rock before their eyes . . . Moses and Aaron gathered the congregation together before the rock." Depending on your sources you can get different totals of the multitude that came out of Egypt. In my research I have come across numbers ranging from three million to more than five million. To make a conservative estimate, I will go even lower and use one million. The question I am concerned about is how big a rock does it take for at least one million people to see it at the same time? If we used those higher numbers, which I think are closer to reality, the rock would have to have been even bigger. What I am saying, "Is anything too hard for God?"

The Great Wrestling Match

Jacob was left alone to contemplate the pending meeting with his estranged brother, Esau. Look at Genesis 32:24, "Jacob was left alone; and there wrestled a man with him until the breaking of the day." If we are to believe Scripture, it plainly says he wrestled a man until the breaking of the day. There is nothing about a spirit. Verse 25: "And when he saw that he prevailed not against him, he touched the hollow of his thigh; and the hollow of Jacob's thigh was out of joint, as he wrestled with him." I would like to inject this bit of irony: we are always at a disadvantage when we wrestle or contend with God. Jacob began to have a conversation with this man as they contended. Verse 26: "And he said, let me go for the day breaketh. And he said I will not let thee go, except thou bless me." I am astonished at this dialog between Jacob and the wrestler. He told Jacob to let him go because the day was breaking. Was that because the light of day would show Jacob something he was not supposed to see? I believe the light of day would have shown Jacob the face of the pre-incarnate Jesus Christ. God has access to any time or place—present, past, or future. Is anything too hard for God? In the latter clause of verse 26, "I will not let thee go except thou bless me" Jacob seemed to have a clear understanding of who he wrestled with, because he asked for a blessing. The blessing came in the form of a name change, a change that only God had the power to give. The new name *Israel* simply means "he who fought with God."

Looking at verse 30: "Jacob called the name of the place Peniel: for I have seen God face to face and my life is preserved." In verse 26, "for the day breaketh," I wonder if Jacobs's life would have been preserved if he had seen God's face in the light of day. Wrestling with God under the cover of darkness concealed the face of God even though Jacob was face to face with God. I mentioned earlier that in the Old Testament Christ is only mentioned, not revealed. Scripture conveys that when the fullness of time had come, God sent His son. However, God does not evolve; He has declared the end from the beginning and He is what He is without ever being what He is not.

Jesus Standing on the Right Hand of God

In Acts 7:55 we find these words, "But he [Stephen] being full of the Holy Ghost, looked up steadfastly into heaven and saw the glory of God and Jesus standing on the right hand of God." The position of standing on the right hand or just the right hand has to do with power, strength, and protection. Look at Psalm 17:7, "Show thy marvelous lovingkindness, O thou that savest by thy right hand, them which put their trust in thee from those that rise up against them." The right hand being the symbol of power, Jesus spoke in Matthew 28:18 saying, "All power is given unto me in heaven and in earth." I interject a question: "If Jesus is not God and according to Scripture has all power in heaven and in earth, where is God's power?" In Psalm 90:2 we find these words of life, "Before the mountains were brought forth, or ever thou hadst formed the earth and the world, even from everlasting to everlasting, thou art God." God has no end because we just read He is from everlasting to everlasting—always was and always will be. If God is everlasting and Jesus is the only one with all power, do you believe Jesus and God are one? Deuteronomy 4:35 brings more light to this subject, "The Lord he is God; there is none else beside him." He shares His throne with no one else. Again I go to Acts 7:56-57: "Behold I see the heavens opened and the son of man [Jesus] standing on the right hand of God . . . then they cried out with a loud voice and stopped their ears and ran upon him with one accord." What they heard from Stephen was that Jesus was in heaven. If indeed Jesus was in heaven—He was and still is—then they had crucified an innocent man. This they could not bear to hear. In verse 59, they stoned Stephen who called upon God, saying "Lord Jesus, receive my spirit." Looking at this verse I can only, through the Holy Ghost, come up with one explanation, that Stephen, being full of the Holy Ghost, identified God as Lord Jesus, and God did not correct him. During his address he asked the Lord Jesus to receive his spirit. To those of you who are blessed to be able to read what God has written, I usher you to Ecclesiastics 12:7: "Then shall the dust return to the earth as it was: and the spirit shall return unto God who gave it." Luke 23:46: "And when Jesus had cried with a loud voice, he said, Father into thy hands I commend my spirit." Exactly what are these scriptures saying? Quite simply, only God can receive departed or disembodied spirits at death. That being true, Stephen said, "Lord Jesus, receive my spirit." The Scripture screams, "Jesus is God!" We look at Acts 7:60 as Stephen is about to leave this world: "And he kneeled down and cried with a loud voice, Lord, lay not this sin to their charge." The words "lay not this sin to their charge" undoubtedly mean do not charge them with this sin. Stephen admits that what they were doing to him was indeed a sin, because he was innocent. Stephen was asking that their sin be forgiven. I call your attention to Isaiah 43:25: "I, even I, am he who blots out your transgressions, for my own sake and remember your sins no more." Luke 5:21—"who can forgive sins, but God alone?" You are probably aware where I am going with this: if only God can forgive sins, why did Stephen ask Jesus not to lay this sin to their charge? Stephen asked Jesus to do what only God could do because Stephen knew Jesus was God.

Summary

I hope what you have just read will jump start your curiosity. What you have just read was merely highlighted scripture that tells us Jesus indeed is the Almighty God. Second Timothy 2:15 reminds us that we are to continue rightly dividing the Word of God. We are to cut it right and walk in the path of truth. We must divide what we think from what God's Word really says. I don't believe anyone, no matter how long they have walked with God, can prove Jesus is God. Therefore, we must rely on God's Word, for therein lies the truth.

I and My Father are one; He who has seen Me has seen the Father. In Jesus dwells all the fullness of the Godhead bodily. What could possibly cause anyone not to understand these quotes? There are two reasons: the first is the lack of an indwelling of the Holy Ghost; the second and more common is not allowing the Holy Ghost to lead you into all truth. First Thessalonians tells us not to quench the Spirit; that is the action we take when we lean on our own understanding, not rightly dividing the Word of truth. It is much easier to teach an unlearned person than one who has already been taught and formed a barrier to new teaching, even if it be the truth. However, the Bible states that the anointing destroys the yoke, and with the Holy Ghost comes the anointing that can make a revelation in a flash.

God Can, God Did, God Will

The spirit of God moved upon the face of the waters
The same spirit was poured out on sons
and daughters

Became a rock that gave water when smote by a rod
Reminding Israel, I am the only true God

Show us the Father, one said, that will suffice
When you see me you see the father, said Christ

Give us Barabbas and crucify this Christ
Our sins were many and would cost a great price

I am the word made flesh and dwelled among men
For the sole purpose of redemption and giving
power over sin

Christ said, all power is given unto me in
heaven and earth
Come unto me all ye that hunger and thirst

GOD A.K.A. JESUS CHRIST

I can stand in a furnace and take the heat
out of the flame
To protect those who stood for me and honored
my name

I can be a cloud by day and fire by night
Whatever it takes to keep my people in the light

In trouble? I can come to you if I have to
walk on water
Without the support of rocks, sand, or mortar

From the bow of a ship I rebuked the wind and
made the sea be still
Because I have all power, everything is subject to
my will

So powerful, no man taketh my life, I lay it down
Pick it up when I get ready; I know where
it can be found

I vetoed the power of the grave, and canceled
death's sting
I have power over anything Satan can bring

I can ascend up on high, because I have ultimate
hang time
Gravity is submissive to me, I formed it, I made it,
it is mine

I can raise a dead man, who has been that way for
three days

GOD A.K.A. JESUS CHRIST

Death is not permanent, for those who love me, it's
only a phase

My body fluids have power, my blood, even my spit
When applied to the tongue will make
the impediment quit

My blood can wash away all your sins
Didn't you know, at the house of God
judgment begins

Live holy and righteous, for soon I will return
To rapture those who love me, others in hell
will burn

On a swift cloud will I come, that is what I ride
To gather my jewels, forever to be by my side

- RSS

Jesus Only, Only Jesus

Jesus only, came by a virgin birth
Only Jesus, knew what men's soul was worth

Jesus only, died for the sins of the world
Only Jesus, for every man, woman, boy, and girl

Jesus only, on the third day rose from the grave
Only Jesus, knew how to speak and
make death behave

Jesus only, under heaven there is no other name
Only Jesus, yesterday, today and forever the same

Jesus only, ascended past all principalities on high
Only Jesus, will return and call his people
from the sky

Jesus only, sits on the throne
Only Jesus, he and he alone

- RSS

Author's Biography

Born, Richard Steven Schofield to Willie and Tanner Schofield, Elder Richard Schofield's life has been anything but Ho-Hum. In 1965 less than a week after his high school graduation in Beckley, WV he departed for New Haven, Ct. To hear him tell it he went seeking fortune, fame and bright lights. The fortune never came, the fame turned to shame and the bright lights barely got above a flicker. Elder Schofield was raised in an apostolic house-hold, and even today he is a third generation apostolic. However, he ran from God for over 14 years, while away from home. He contends his experience with drugs, being homeless and just the sin experience itself makes him ever grateful for the saving power of God. Elder Schofield maintains the turning point in his life came late one night after engulfing marijuana and lying down. Elder Schofield reveals that he heard a voice say "what are you doing up here in Connecticut. He immediately sat straight up in bed, looked around the room to see who was there, he saw no one. This voice came a second time a few days later and still he saw no one. Elder Schofield said at that time he chalked the experience up to the effects of the high he was on at that time. However shortly there after (a matter of weeks) he boarded a train headed back home to West Virginia. He arrived home in May of 1979; God saved him in October of the same year. After some years of walking with God, Elder Schofield says God revealed unto him that it was him (God) who asked the question "what are you doing up here in Connecticut?" Elder Schofield has been married to the captivating Rometta Hawkins Schofield for the past 26 years, which he calls the best years of his life. Rometta blessed him with Stephanie and Richard II his two children of whom he says were surely a God send.

Contact author:
godakajc@sbcglobal.net

www.ingramcontent.com/pod-product-compliance
Ingram Content Group UK Ltd.
Pitfield, Milton Keynes, MK11 3LW, UK
UKHW041943230426
12048UKWH00008B/107